Original title:
Every Breath With You

Copyright © 2024 Creative Arts Management OÜ
All rights reserved.

Author: Natalie Nelson
ISBN HARDBACK: 978-9908-0-0904-9
ISBN PAPERBACK: 978-9908-0-0905-6

Paths Intertwined

In the park, we dance like fools,
Chasing squirrels and breaking rules.
Your laughter echoes, a silly song,
With you beside me, nothing feels wrong.

We trip on grass and giggle loud,
Cracking jokes, making fun of the crowd.
You wink, I snort, it's quite a sight,
Our silly antics, pure delight.

With ice cream splatters on our shirts,
We play tag and dodge the dirt.
You steal my fries without a blame,
But I love you more; it's all a game.

Through winding paths, we roam and ramble,
Creating chaos, like an unruly scramble.
In this crazy life, you're my best friend,
Together forever, let the laughter never end.

The Essence of Connection

In the midst of chaos, you find me there,
With socks that don't match, oh, what a pair!
Your laughter like jelly, it wiggles and shakes,
We dance in our kitchen, making mistakes.

When you trip on your words, it's a sight so sweet,
We giggle like kids, on sugar, in heat.
Planting our goofy, delightful little seeds,
Together we thrive, yes, that's all we need.

Tides of Togetherness

Like waves that come crashing, we splash and we play,
Building our castles, just to wash them away.
You steal all my fries, I pretend not to care,
But deep down, my stomach does a happy dance there.

As we chase seagulls while wearing odd hats,
We share all the crumbs with curious cats.
Under the sun, with goofy grins wide,
Ocean of laughter, it's where we abide.

Harmony in the Unsaid

With you, all my secrets feel safe in a whisper,
Like socks on a hamster, or pizza with blister.
The looks that we share, they can say it all,
In a world full of chaos, together we sprawl.

When silence is golden, we still want the snacks,
Your snorts and your giggles are my favorite acts.
A symphony plays, with rhythms so sweet,
In our little bubble, we dance to our beat.

In This Sacred Space

In our cozy little corner, where chaos takes flight,
We've crafted a kingdom of joy, pure delight.
With pillow-fort castles and snacks piled high,
We conquer the world, you and I, oh my!

As we dream up adventures that never unfold,
You tell me the tales that will never get old.
With hiccups and antics, our spirits ignite,
In this sacred space, all feels just right.

Floating on a Sea of Moments

We sail on jokes and silly dreams,
With laughter echoing like sunlit beams.
A splash of whimsy, a wave of cheer,
In our boat of nonsense, there's nothing to fear.

Bobbing along on this goofy tide,
Your quirks are treasures I can't hide.
We paddle through giggles and friendly tease,
Together we float, it's a breeze of ease.

Pulse of Togetherness

Our hearts beat funny in a goofy dance,
With silly rhythms, we take a chance.
A thump of laughter, a shimmy on cue,
You bring the spice to my oh-so-dry stew.

We sync our chuckles like a metronome,
Creating a ruckus in our cozy home.
With each shared pun, our spirits ignite,
In this comedy show, we're stars of the night.

Where Time Meets Heartbeat

Time tickles us like a playful cat,
As we chase moments while wearing a hat.
With winks and nudges, we giggle and play,
In this hilarity, we'll never stray.

Each second together is a laughter spree,
Like popcorn popping, just wait and see.
We're two clowns in a circus of fate,
Mastering the art of love, oh so great.

Under the Weight of Shared Wishes

We carry dreams like a feathered pack,
With wishes so light, there's no looking back.
Arm in arm, we stumble and trip,
But, oh, how we giggle, it's quite a trip!

With every huff and puff we share,
Life's a big laugh, with stories to spare.
In the weight of our hopes, we dance and sway,
Making wishes together, come what may.

Love's Quiet Song

Your snoring sounds like thunder,
Yet I find it quite a wonder.
You steal the sheets with flair,
But I wouldn't swap this air.

In the kitchen, you try to bake,
Last time, we had quite the quake!
Flour flying through the air,
I laughed till I cried, I swear!

Secrets in the Breeze

Whispers carried through the trees,
Like you sneezing, oh, such a tease!
Your laugh, a melody so sweet,
Even if it sounds like a beat.

Secrets shared with goofy grins,
You've got that charm, it always wins.
When you trip, oh what a sight,
We both roll around with delight!

Moments Woven in Time

Our first date was a pizza mess,
You spilled on me, I must confess.
Sauce down my shirt, oh what a crime,
Yet with you, I'd do it every time.

Walking home, you tried to dance,
You tripped again, but took a chance.
With every twist, my heart would chime,
In silly moments, we craft our rhyme.

A Connection Beyond Words

You make faces like a clown,
Whenever I feel a bit down.
Your silly jokes, they never fail,
Together, we write our own tale.

In silly selfies, we capture bliss,
Who knew a wink could feel like this?
With each laughter, our fun unfurls,
In our odd world, I found my pearls.

Tethered in Time

In a world where socks can hide,
We laugh as we take life in stride.
You missed the bus, I spilled my drink,
Yet somehow, it's more fun than we think.

With your hair like birds in flight,
We argue if it's day or night.
You wear my shoes, I wear your hat,
A photo op, where's the cat?

Every sandwich shared is a dream,
Your mustard skills are quite the theme.
We swap our stories, one by one,
Turning chores into a game of fun.

So here's to us, a silly pair,
Our laughter floating in the air.
In chaos, joy finds its space,
With quirks that time cannot erase.

Murmurs of our Souls

Whispers carried on the breeze,
Your goofy dance brings me to my knees.
We serenade the laundry pile,
And wear each other's shirts with style.

You sneak a snack while I distract,
In this wild life, there's no pact.
Pillow fights and late-night chats,
Our friendship's like those silly hats.

Every secret shared is a thrill,
With you, my heart can never chill.
Like clowns in socks, we tumble and spin,
Together, that's where the fun begins.

So let's laugh until we cry,
And chase the stars across the sky.
Our souls may murmur, but our hearts sing,
In this circus, we're the real king.

Chords of Affection

In a jam session of silly tunes,
We dance like butterflies in June.
You strum my heart, I play your mind,
In this concert, our quirks unwind.

With puns that echo through the air,
We wear the strangest outfits with flair.
You mock my laugh, I laugh twice as loud,
In our little world, we are so proud.

Each note we play a funny tale,
Like kites that tangle in the gale.
In silly lyrics, we find the way,
To turn mundane into a play.

Together, we strum, we pluck, we play,
With chords of affection that never fray.
In this orchestra of mirth and cheer,
Every note strikes joy, that much is clear.

Gentle Touch of Existence

In gentle nudges of morning light,
We stumble through the day with delight.
Your coffee spills on my new shirt,
But together, who cares about dirt?

Tickling ribs with mischievous grin,
Our silly games begin to spin.
You trip on air, and I just stare,
Laughter erupts, beyond compare.

Side by side on this merry ride,
With you, there's never a need to hide.
Our little quirks are treasures to greet,
Turning simple moments into a treat.

Hand in hand, we explore the scene,
Chasing dreams where we've never been.
In this gentle touch of crazy fun,
Together, forever, we're never done.

The Garden of Us

In the garden where we play,
Sunflowers dance, come what may.
You trip on roots, I laugh so loud,
Bees buzz around like a cheering crowd.

With watering cans, we cause a splash,
You claim it's art, I call it trash.
Tulips gossip, petals in a whirl,
Our antics make the daisies twirl.

When veggies argue, we stand in awe,
Who knew a carrot could make a law?
We chuckle as the weeds throw shade,
In our little world, absurd but made.

So here's to growing through laughter and strife,
In the garden we've painted, full of life.
With every pruning and silly noise,
We cultivate joy, our eternal poise.

Dreams Encased in Time

In dreams we float like clouds of fluff,
Building castles, oh, aren't they tough?
You sprout wings, I fly like a kite,
But trip on clouds, oh, what a sight!

Time ticks by, we giggle and race,
Chasing shadows, a whimsical chase.
You trip on stardust, what a mess,
We laugh till we cry, what a success!

With clocks that melt and cheese on toast,
We toast to dreams, now that's the most!
In slippers we roam through wonderland,
With wobbly joy, hand in hand.

So let's dance between the ticks and tocks,
In dreams encased in mismatched socks.
With every tick, I'm glad you're mine,
In this comedic realm, we simply shine.

A Harmony of Heartbeats

We dance like two offbeat clowns,
In rhythm with our silly frowns.
Your left foot goes right, mine does a twist,
In this waltz of joy, how could we resist?

Our heartbeats sync with a quirky beat,
Like jazz hands in a baker's suite.
You bake a cake, I frost it blue,
Who knew desserts could play peek-a-boo?

With spoons that clang and laughter bright,
We stir up mischief in the moonlight.
Every giggle's a note, a swell,
In our symphony, we cast our spell.

So let's serenade the stars above,
As we compose this tune of love.
In a harmony where fun thrives,
With each silly moment, our heartbeats jive.

Whispers Beneath the Moon

Beneath the moon, we share our plots,
Silly secrets and giggle spots.
You say the stars have silly names,
Like Bob and Larry, oh what games!

The crickets chirp a tune of jest,
In this moonlit hour, we're truly blessed.
You dance with shadows, a sly old fox,
While the moon rolls its eyes at our paradox.

With whispers soft, we paint the night,
In wobbly tales, our dreams take flight.
You tickle my ear, a playful tease,
And laughter twirls in the midnight breeze.

So here we roam, mischief our guide,
With every chuckle, my heart's wide.
In moonlit whispers, we forge our way,
Through the fun and the laughter, come what may.

Whispers in the Air

In the park, we dance and prance,
Taking twirls, giving laughter a chance.
Your goofy grin, oh what a sight,
The squirrels stare, caught in our light.

We share secrets, chocolate and fries,
You tell a joke, and I nearly cry.
The wind carries giggles, up so high,
As we chase shadows, letting time fly.

Moments Between Heartbeats

Waiting in line, you poke my side,
My face turns red, a funny ride.
You mime a fish, flopping about,
The grumpy lady gives a pout.

In the café, we spill our drinks,
I snort my laugh, and the barista blinks.
Your wiggle dance tickles my heart,
In the laughter, we'll never part.

Inhale the Magic of Togetherness

Our socks don't match, who needs that flair?
You wear a hat like a fluffy bear.
The sparkles fly when you lose your shoe,
I trip over giggles, and fall too.

Bubbles and laughter, the silly kind,
You tickle me, I've lost my mind.
We toast with soda on a sunny day,
In our weird world, we're here to stay.

Silent Spaces

In the silence, I hear your grin,
Sipping our soda, it's a win-win.
You pull a face, and my heart skips,
The secret language of silly quips.

With winks and nudges, we float in bliss,
Those quiet chuckles, oh what I miss.
You reach for popcorn, it's flying high,
A soaring snack, we laugh and sigh.

Shared Souls

You tell a tale, I roll my eyes,
But then you trip, oh what a surprise!
The way you stumble, it melts my heart,
In this show, we both play a part.

We race our shadows down the street,
With silly dances, we must compete.
Our hearts connected, it feels so bright,
In this crazy world, you're my delight.

Floating on Warmth

In sunlight's glow, we sway and spin,
With ice cream cones that melt like sin.
You steal my fries, I feign a frown,
But laughter bubbles, up and down.

A picnic dream on this bright space,
You trip on air, and I lose grace.
We chase the clouds, pretend to fly,
And giggle hard, oh my, oh my!

Echoes of Our Laughter

In silly games, we take the lead,
You call it fun, I call it greed.
With jokes so bad, we roll on floors,
A symphony of snorts and roars.

From tickles here to playful shoves,
You're my partner in all the loves.
In echoes sweet, our joy does climb,
Punchlines shared, we're out of time!

Dance of Shared Silence

We sit together, silent cheer,
With snacks in hand, who needs a beer?
Your awkward grin, a strange delight,
In friendly silence, hearts ignite.

A wink exchanged, we start to grin,
You mock my dance, and I move in.
With every glance, our joy expands,
In awkward steps, we make our plans!

Threads of Us

Stitching moments, make them neat,
With yarns of laughter, bittersweet.
We weave our tales, both wild and bold,
In threads of us, together sewn.

With mismatched socks and quirky hats,
You're all the fun in silly spats.
In each odd thread, a story grows,
A blanket warm, our friendship glows!

Inhale the Quiet

In the stillness of the night,
I hear your snore, what a delight.
A symphony of sleepy sounds,
While the world spins round and round.

The cat jumps up and thumps my head,
As you're dreaming, sweetly, instead.
I try to breathe in all the peace,
But I giggle; it's a funny feast.

Close my eyes and just pretend,
That this noise is my best friend.
Each puff of air brings laughs so near,
In the quiet, it's all crystal clear.

So here we lie, like two old clowns,
With puffs and giggles as our crowns.
In silent breaths, our joy takes flight,
Every chuckle fills the night.

Exhaled Secrets

In the moment's hush, I share,
A secret that we both must bear.
A little chuckle, a soft roar,
As I whisper, 'You've snored before!'

Floating words like bubbles pop,
As each one wobbles, won't you stop?
The silly games we play at night,
Making even silence feel so bright.

Your laughter blends with my own sighs,
In this duet, truth never lies.
Secrets spilled like milk, what fun,
In these moments, we are one.

While stars above start to conspire,
We laugh as dreams fuel our desire.
With each exhale, secrets spread,
In our world of joy, we tread.

Pulse of Our Connection

Between each giggle, hearts collide,
Life's funny rhythm, we can't hide.
Tapping toes and wiggly chairs,
Together, we make silly pairs.

A beat of laughter fills the room,
Our pulses thump, dispelling gloom.
We dance around the kitchen tray,
In this rhythm, we find our way.

With ice cream tubs and cookie crumbs,
Heartbeats mix with silly hums.
In every pulse, a joke is spun,
In our jester's world, we're always fun.

So let's embrace this wacky beat,
Our pulses race, no missed heartbeat.
In the silly moments that connect,
Laughter is our perfect effect.

Heartbeats in Harmony

Two hearts that dance a crazy jig,
Like rubber ducks on strings so big.
In this chaotic, joyful spree,
Our heartbeats hum in harmony.

Each thump a laugh, each skip a grin,
In this life, where do we begin?
With wacky whims, we jive through the day,
Turning mundane times into play.

In the kitchen, oh what a mess,
We bubble and giggle, nothing less.
With pots and pans, we clash and clang,
In our duet, the world must sang.

So here we are, in perfect tune,
Making mischief morning to noon.
Our heartbeats' rhythm, a funny show,
In laughter's glow, we truly grow.

Chasing the Fragrance of You

In the garden, scents collide,
Petals giggle, blooms take pride.
I chased a whiff, got led astray,
My nose might smell more than I say.

Butterflies dance with joyful glee,
While bees tease your sweet decree.
I stumble, spill, a clumsy muse,
Trying to catch those fragrant views.

Unfolding Stories in Stillness

In silence, tales begin to play,
A wink, a grin, a bright bouquet.
Our voices hush, the world slows down,
Each giggle wrapped in laughter's crown.

Time quivers, tickles the nose,
As popcorn fumbles and laughter flows.
We unravel laughs, one by one,
In stillness, our stories become fun.

Threads of Air

Whispers twirl like threads so fine,
Dancing lightly, yours and mine.
We weave a tapestry of cheer,
Each thread stitched with love we steer.

Airy jokes float up so high,
Tickling clouds that pass us by.
In each gust, a shared surprise,
Brightening the skies like fireflies.

Ties of Love

Our snickers twist like playful ties,
Each quip and jest, a sweet reprise.
With every knot, we knot our fate,
Silly moments that can't be late.

Tangled laughs and joyful cries,
In this bond, nobody sighs.
We're bound by giggles, hearts aglow,
Truths hidden in humor's flow.

The Language of Our Laughter

Your laugh speaks volumes, so loud, so clear,
With every joke, we conquer fear.
In giggles and snorts, our souls connect,
The language we share, so perfect, unchecked.

A hiccup here, a snicker there,
In our dialogue, we have flair.
With puns like clouds, we take to flight,
In hilarity's arms, we shine so bright.

The Rhythm of Us

In the dance of our daily grind,
You step on my toes, but that's just fine.
We twirl through mornings, coffee in hand,
Your laughter's the beat, my favorite band.

We stumble through grocery aisles so bright,
You reach for the snacks, oh what a sight!
With each little misstep, we giggle and sway,
Your quirks are a melody, brightening my day.

Echoes of Our Shared Silence

In quiet moments, we sit side by side,
Me munching on chips, you safe in your pride.
The silence we share is loud as a drum,
With your quirky glances, you make me go numb.

As we binge-watch shows, lost in our zone,
Your humor's a comfort, like pizza on loan.
We laugh at the plots, oh what a delight,
In the echoes of silence, everything feels right.

In the Embrace of Time's Flow

Time trickles slowly, like molasses on toast,
Yet here with your antics, I cherish the most.
Each tick of the clock, a jest we create,
While you wear your socks that totally don't mate.

We stroll through the park, my umbrella your hat,
With sunshine and giggles, who could be flat?
Each moment we scrap, oh the joy that we reap,
In the embrace of time, our laughter won't sleep.

Currents of Love Unseen

Beneath all the chaos, your smile is a spark,
Like finding a treasure while roaming in the dark.
Each quirk that you flaunt is a wave in the tide,
On this funny adventure, it's you by my side.

With silly jokes whispered, we float like a dream,
In currents of joy, we're the perfect team.
Through life's little quirks, our laughter's the glue,
In this wild little journey, I'm so glad it's with you.

A Symphony of Two

In a kitchen dance, we trip and slide,
Spaghetti flops, there's nowhere to hide.
You sing off-key, I laugh so loud,
Together we make the silliest crowd.

The dog joins in, a howling friend,
A duet's born, it has no end.
With pots as drums, and spoons for flair,
In our little band, we have not a care.

The neighbors peek, with puzzled eyes,
Wondering if laughter is our disguise.
In our silly world, we find the tune,
Making sweet music by the light of the moon.

A symphony of fun, with you I sway,
In every blunder, we find our way.
So let the chaos and giggles ensue,
Life is a concert, just me and you.

Underneath the Stars

We lay on grass, counting each light,
You giggle and say, 'Is that one bright?'
A shooting star whizzes on by,
You make a wish, and I start to cry.

Not for the wish, but your goofy face,
Laughter spills over, filling the space.
We plot schemes for intergalactic escape,
Dressed as aliens, we laugh and gape.

Your toe pokes mine, a ticklish fight,
We roll and tumble, pure delight.
In this celestial dance beneath the skies,
Magic unfolds in our silly highs.

So here we are, in this cosmic spree,
A comedy duo, just you and me.
Under stars so bright, with giggles shared,
In this universe, love is declared.

Gentle Waves of Affection

On the beach, we jump with glee,
Splashing water, just you and me.
You toss a wave, I pretend to dive,
Each silly moment makes us feel alive.

Building castles, they tumble down,
You wear sand like a quirky crown.
Seagulls laugh, they join our spree,
In this sandy fun, we're wild and free.

With every wave, our laughter breaks,
An ocean of joy, no room for lakes.
Sunsets paint our goofy smiles,
In this beachside play, we stretch the miles.

As the tide rolls in, we dance and sway,
In the ebb and flow, we find our way.
Gentle waves of joy, we ride anew,
Silly rhythms, just me and you.

Together in Stillness

In comfy chairs, we sit side by side,
Sharing snacks, in laughter we glide.
You snort at jokes, I spill my drink,
In our cozy chaos, we hardly think.

The world outside can zoom and race,
But here with you, there's no need for haste.
We binge on shows, critique the plot,
Why is it funny? We know not!

Your quirky dance when the credits roll,
A funny little sketch, that's your goal.
With snacks all tossed, and laughter bright,
In this stillness, everything feels right.

Together we dwell in our little nest,
In the funny stillness, we're truly blessed.
Every moment counts, in joy we bask,
In our stillness shared, all I do is ask.

A Symphony of Life's Exhale

In the grand orchestra of our days,
We play the notes in silly ways.
Clumsy waltz upon the floor,
You drop your cake, I want some more.

We laugh and tumble, laugh and fall,
Chasing echoes down the hall.
Each giggle spills like soda pop,
We're both just glad we never stop.

With every hiccup, every cheer,
Our friendship's melody is clear.
High notes buzzing, low notes sway,
In this concert, we're here to play.

So grab your kazoo, here's the cue,
Let's make our tunes all bright and new.
Together we'll create a sound,
Life's best symphony we've found.

Touching the Essence of Now

Fingers sticky from the ice cream,
We laugh until we almost scream.
The world spins on, but here we stand,
In a moment that's perfectly unplanned.

A burst of giggles, then a snort,
Sudden hiccups, a funny sport.
You throw a wink, I roll my eyes,
This sweet chaos, a grand surprise.

Frisbees flying, dogs askew,
These little things make life brand new.
Jumping puddles, splashing free,
What a sight—just you and me!

Tickle fights and silly quotes,
Riding waves on lazy boats.
Each moment glimmers, shines, and glows,
In our crazy, joyful show.

Gathering Clouds of Shared Dreams

Underneath the fluffy skies,
We gather dreams like paper flies.
With a grin, you toss them high,
Till one floats down with a goofy sigh.

Sock puppets dance upon the bed,
With silly voices, we're lightly led.
A fleet of clouds, we drift and beam,
Together charting this wild dream.

You've got a notion; I've got a scheme,
Mixing colors like a sweet ice cream.
We paint our visions, bright and bold,
In this world, we'll watch them unfold.

Rain or shine, we'll take the ride,
With laughter bubbling deep inside.
So let's gather clouds, no need to fuss,
In this silly dream, just you and us.

Dance of Synchronized Hearts

Two left feet upon the floor,
Every misstep makes us roar.
Twisting, turning, who can tell?
In this dance, we know it well.

You lead with laughter, I follow the fun,
Chasing shadows made by the sun.
With silly steps, we skip and prance,
Two goofy souls in a happy dance.

Each twirl's a giggle, each spin's a cheer,
A waltz of quirks, and that's quite clear.
Our hearts keep rhythm, a jolly beat,
In this crazy party, we can't be beat.

So hold my hand and let's unite,
In this odd ballet, day and night.
With hearts in sync, let's be absurd,
Together we'll leap like hummingbirds.

In the Presence of You

In the room, you always snore,
Rattling windows, shakes the floor.
I wave my hand, I shout your name,
You roll and grin, it's all a game.

Your laugh is like a bubbling brook,
These silly moments, take a look.
With popcorn fights and silly jokes,
Life's a circus, we're the folks.

Side by side, we make a mess,
Cooking's chaos, I confess.
While flour flies and pots all clank,
Who knew love was this wacky prank?

So here's to us, a quirky pair,
Stumbling through life without a care.
With you, my dear, it's humor's blend,
In this madness, I've found my friend.

Synchronized Souls

You dance like a chicken in the rain,
While I attempt to hide my pain.
But here we are, in this wild spin,
Two left feet, let the fun begin!

We wear mismatched socks with pride,
Giggles bubble, we cannot hide.
Your silly faces steal my heart,
In this great show, you play your part.

Pajama parties, popcorn thrills,
Late-night snacks, more giggles spill.
We share our dreams in whispered tones,
Knowing well, we're not alone.

With synchronized blunders, we shine bright,
Hand in hand, we own the night.
Together, we wave the world goodbye,
In our own comedy, meant to fly.

Sunlight on Our Path

Morning light spills on your bedhead,
I chuckle softly, can't help but spread.
You strike a pose, all goofy grace,
Our lives, my love, a funny chase.

Coffee spills, you blame the cat,
We sip and laugh, how about that?
Sunshine dances in our eyes,
Each moment shared, a sweet surprise.

You trip on air, oh, what a sight!
I laugh so hard, it feels just right.
With you, I find my silly muse,
In all our stumbles, it's joy we choose.

So let's wander where the sun shines bright,
In a world of giggles, pure delight.
Hand in hand, we'll sail this day,
Laughing our troubles all away.

Reflections in the Twilight

As the sun dips, shadows grow long,
We chase the whispers of our song.
You're a silly ghost, I'm a friendly shade,
In this silly dance, memories are made.

With nightfall's laugh, we share our dreams,
Riddles and jokes in moonlight beams.
Your goofy grin is all I need,
In this twilight, our hearts succeed.

We build our kingdom out of stars,
Laughing 'bout deficits in our cars.
The moon winks down on our foolish pride,
In every moment, joy's our guide.

So raise a toast to our antics grand,
In twilight's glow, we take our stand.
With laughter echoing into the night,
Our love's the punchline, shining bright.

Through Clouds of Serendipity

We float on air, just like a kite,
With giggles loud, our moods so bright.
Chasing clouds that waddle by,
Like fluffy sheep in a big blue sky.

You spill your drink, I spill my snack,
We laugh so hard, can't hold back.
A twirl, a skip, we dance with glee,
In this silly world, just you and me.

Carried by the Wind's Secret

On a breeze of laughter, we glide along,
Making up tunes, inventing our song.
Tickling the trees, cracking a joke,
The fun in our chatter, like the sun it soaks.

You wore mismatched shoes today,
I laughed so hard, I lost my way.
With silly hats and quirky ties,
Our friendship sparkles under laughing skies.

Counting Moments in Private Spaces

In hidden nooks, we spin our tales,
With giggly whispers, and exaggerated wails.
A treasure hunt for candy and sweets,
Each moment shared feels like a feast.

With finger puppets, we put on a play,
Dancing like goofballs every day.
Counting laughs like we count the stars,
Building our dreams under moonlit bars.

Light of Hearts

We glow like lanterns in the dark,
With jokes that land like a comical lark.
Each moment shines, a twinkling spree,
In the joy of your smile, I feel so free.

Like fireflies darting, silly and bright,
We dance through the playground, pure delight.
Sharing secrets like candy cane bliss,
This silly friendship, you don't want to miss.

Shadows of Night

In shadows grey, we find our joy,
Making up games with a simple toy.
Whispering secrets under the trees,
Giggling quietly, just you and me.

Starlight winking plays tricks on the eyes,
Telling tall tales that rival the skies.
We race in the dark like silly pups,
In the giggle-filled night, nothing stops us.

Mesmerizing Every Minute

In the morning, you spill coffee,
The dog gives you the stink eye.
We laugh as you trip on the floor,
And the cat watches with a sigh.

Your dance moves, oh so bizarre,
They make me snort with delight.
Twisting and turning, a true star,
In our kitchen, under moonlight.

You say socks are your fashion skill,
I question your choice of style.
But as you strut, with humor to fill,
I can't help but laugh all the while.

Time with you is a goofy ride,
With all the quirks that you bring.
Through chuckles and laughter, I glide,
How lucky I am, you're my thing.

The Pulse of Togetherness

On Wednesdays, we play silly games,
You try to make me laugh the loudest.
Your jokes are often quite insane,
But who could ever doubt the proudest?

Silly faces in the mirror,
You pull a grin to crack me up.
As you approach, I feel the cheer,
In our colorful, wacky cup.

Dinner plans are quite the jest,
You cook while wearing a chef's hat.
With every burn, I must confess,
I adore our kitchen combat.

In the quiet, when the day fades,
You share jokes that make me snicker.
So thankful for these charming parades,
Life with you just keeps getting quicker.

Shades of Our Love

You pick the wildest colors today,
Clashing socks and polka dots.
Each outfit is a grand ballet,
Turns the mundane into hot spots.

Sipping tea, you spill a bit,
On my nose, a charming sight.
Odd, silly moments, never quit,
That's the spark of our delight.

Your puns, they always land with flair,
I can't escape; I'm in too deep.
Through giggles, I sit back and stare,
These hues of love, my heart does keep.

In quirky ways, you touch the soul,
With laughter echoing around.
You make the silly feeling whole,
In shades of joy, we're forever bound.

Flowing Through Time

With clocks that tick, we dance and sway,
The past has got nothing on us.
Can't recall why we laughed today,
But we both know it's all a plus.

Through tickles and playful nudges,
We race to the fridge for a bite.
You drag me into the fun trudges,
Like kids at a carnival night.

Every glance has its own funny tale,
As we wear this giggle crown.
With love as our ship, we set sail,
Floating, we never look down.

When twilight whispers, we find more runs,
Chasing each other, come what may.
In this connection where laughter runs,
Time spins, and we seize the day.

Memories Carried in the Wind

In a breeze, I found my hat,
You snagged it, oh, how we laughed!
Chasing dreams on a flying mat,
Life's silly scenes, our own craft.

With the kite that danced so high,
You tugged, and I nearly fell flat!
We waved to clouds draped in the sky,
Our giggles wrapped around that chat.

Every trip brings a brand-new scheme,
From pancakes to a wild raccoon,
In this crazy life, we're a team,
Eating ice cream under the moon.

Oh, the tales that meet the air,
From mishaps that became pure gold!
With you, my dear, I have no cares,
In laughter, our story unfolds.

Heartstrings Entwined

You strummed my heart, like a guitar,
On notes of cheese and silly puns.
With every chord, we've wandered far,
Like kids, we danced and weighed a ton.

In our duet, the cat joins in,
A chaotic but charming sound!
Each little quirk, a cheeky grin,
With tangled strings, love's tightly wound.

When you steal my fries, and I pout,
You offer me the last hot wing!
In this version of love, no doubt,
Our shenanigans make my heart sing.

With a wink and a goofy pose,
Our hearts are tied with every jest.
We're silly, but our laughter grows,
A bond that always feels the best.

Anchored in Your Presence

Like shipmates lost in a silly tide,
You ship-wreck my thoughts with delight!
In your presence, I find a ride,
Together, we'll take on the night.

Your laugh's the anchor, steady and strong,
Through waves of chaos, we find our way.
Adventures start with our silly song,
As seaweed dances in bright ballet.

With treasure maps drawn on napkin notes,
We seek the snacks lurking everywhere!
Chart our course as we plot our boats,
We'll dive in with humor; hearts bare.

Anchored in each other's smile,
Through playful jests, we float with ease.
In this ocean of life, hear us dial,
You and I, the finest of seas!

Moments that Resonate

In a flash, we capture the night,
With flamingo socks worn on parade.
Every misstep, pure delight,
In snapshots of fun, our plans made.

When you dance like no one is near,
Twisting like spaghetti on the floor!
With laughter ringing loud and clear,
We spin through moments, always more.

With spilled drinks and birthday cake fights,
Every moment seems to ignite.
A parade of smiles, no end in sight,
With you, clumsy joy feels just right.

Each slip of the tongue turns to gold,
In echoes of laughter, we find our place.
Through every tale, fondly retold,
Our hearts resonate in humor's embrace.

Notes in the Silence

In the quiet, I hear a sneeze,
Your jokes echo, like a breeze.
Laughter dances, light and free,
Life's a show, just you and me.

Whispers of giggles in the air,
You pretend, oh so unaware.
A muffin falls, crumbs everywhere,
We both just sit and laugh with flair.

Silent stares grow loud and bright,
You slip on socks, a comical sight.
Two clowns beneath the moonlit sky,
Our love's a jest that never says goodbye.

In this pause, a melody sings,
Of silly hearts and little things.
Notes in silence, oh so sweet,
Life with you, is quite the treat.

The Beauty of Being

Here we stand, in mismatched socks,
Your quirks shine brighter than gold clocks.
Every glance a little tease,
The beauty of us, sure to please.

We dance like jelly, wobbly but bold,
Spinning tales, goofy and old.
You laugh so hard, a snort escapes,
Together we're two silly shapes.

We trip over dreams, never a fall,
In puddles of giggles, we've got it all.
Life's a canvas, painted with fun,
Creating chaos, but we have won.

With you, it's like a circus play,
Clowns of love, come what may.
Each silly moment a treasure's gleam,
In the beauty of being, we dream.

Between the Spaces

Between the words, a wink does hide,
A playful secret, joy applied.
Our silence sparks, like magic tricks,
Two captives of quirky little quirks.

In the gaps of chatter, laughter swells,
You tell a joke, how your stomach quells.
Filling air with playful sighs,
Our silent comedy, no need for lies.

The space between can make us grin,
A shared glance, that state we're in.
We laugh at nothing, yet it's all real,
Creating memories that we both feel.

In the pauses, friendship grows,
Between the spaces, joy freely flows.
Moments shared, a treasure to find,
In quiet laughter, we're intertwined.

The Colors of Our Journey

With each trip, we paint the town,
Crayons out when we're feeling down.
You wear red, and I wear blue,
Together we're a vibrant hue.

In this canvas, splashes we make,
Every stumble, a laugh we stake.
Mismatched socks on our endless quest,
Our colorful life is truly the best.

Like a rainbow after the rain,
You bring sunshine, easing the pain.
With every turn and every mile,
Life's a palette with your style.

Through shades and tones of every kind,
In this adventure, our hearts aligned.
The colors of laughter, joy in bloom,
With you, there's never any gloom.

Daydreams Sparked by You

In a cafe, I see you grin,
Butterflies dance, chaos spins.
Sugar spills, laughter flies,
Chocolate syrup, oh what a surprise!

With each giggle, daydreams bloom,
Jellybeans hide in the room.
You juggle donuts, what a scene,
Life's a circus, sweet and keen!

A wink from you, I trip on air,
Thoughts of you, everywhere.
Chasing clouds, I lose my shoe,
In this fun house, it's only us two.

So let's tumble, laugh, and play,
In our world, let's drift away.
With silly quirks, we'll dance and prance,
In our daydreams, let's take a chance!

Imprints of Us in the Night.

Under the stars, we find our groove,
Moonlit shadows, making our moves.
Footprints left in silly shoes,
Dance like nobody, with joyful views.

In the dark, your jokes ignite,
Tickles and giggles, pure delight.
We're two clowns in a cosmic show,
With every laugh, our spirits glow.

The night is young, let's spin around,
With silly dances, off the ground.
You trip on air, I can't contain,
Laughter echoes, a sweet refrain.

Look at the stars, they shine so bright,
They're jealous of our silly plight.
With each moment, we paint the skies,
Imprints of us, in sweet surprise!

Whispers in the Air

A playful breeze carries your cheer,
I hear your laughter, oh so clear.
Like bubbles floating, light as air,
With every whisper, I have to stare.

In secret corners, our giggles collide,
Tickling whispers that can't be denied.
With a wink and a nod, you tease,
Our little secrets bring me to my knees.

Clouds play tag in the sunny skies,
While you toss candy, oh what a surprise!
In this world, nothing feels tight,
Our hearts take flight, pure delight.

So hold my hand, let's run and spin,
Chasing the echoes, let the fun begin.
In the whispers that dance in the air,
Is a world where joy is everywhere!

Moments of Tenderness

In a cozy nook, we plot our schemes,
Crafty capers, like playful dreams.
With puppy eyes and cheeky grins,
Our little antics, where fun begins.

Mismatched socks, a fashion statement,
You lose your hat, what a splendent!
We laugh so hard we start to cry,
In this silly world, we can fly.

Every moment, a treasure we find,
With tickles and hugs, soft and entwined.
Your silly faces, a joyful display,
In our moments, who needs to play?

So let's grab life with a squeeze and a twist,
In the garden of laughter, we coexist.
With our shenanigans, let's never stop,
In the tender moments, we reach for the top!

Ripples in Our Stillness

In a quiet room, you made a sound,
A squeaky chair, what a joy I found.
Our laughs echo, like pings of a bell,
In our stillness, it's easy to tell.

Your dance moves are truly bizarre,
Like a cat that just spotted a car.
I can't help but chuckle each time you sway,
In this silliness, let's just play.

A snack attack in the middle of night,
You stole my fries; oh, what a fright!
With silly faces, we munch and we crunch,
Creating chaos with every lunch.

The calm and the chaos make quite a pair,
With you around, I've no time for despair.
Ripples of laughter, our hearts in a dance,
In the stillness, we find our romance.

Love's Invisible Thread

We're tied together by strings of delight,
Like two stubborn socks that won't take flight.
You steal the covers; I need them to snore,
Yet I snicker, 'cause I love you more.

In the kitchen, you attempt to cook,
The smoke alarm gives quite the look.
With each burnt toast, my heart still sings,
Love's invisible thread ties together odd things.

We argue over who left the cap off the paste,
But laughter wins; it isn't a race.
Your silly puns, they crack me up,
In each little jab, I find the best cup.

We're the dream team — a quirky little pair,
Finding joy in the mundane with flair.
Invisible threads weave laughter and fun,
In this silly dance, we're always one.

Gardens of Togetherness

In our garden, weeds sprout with pride,
You claim they're flowers, with eyes open wide.
We water the plants with giggles and glee,
In this patch of chaos, it's just you and me.

Sunflowers bow to our funny routine,
Dancing in circles, a light-hearted scene.
You whisper to daisies, I roll my eyes,
But laughter blooms under sunny skies.

Each vegetable planted is simply a jest,
Last week it was carrots; today it's a pest.
Yet amongst the greens, our laughter thrives,
In this garden of joy, where friendship survives.

We toss seeds of banter, they scatter like dreams,
While we chase butterflies through sunlight beams,
In each patch of silliness, we sprout anew,
Finding joy in the dirt—my favorite view.

The Light Between Us

There's a spark when we share a glance,
Like fireflies caught in a clumsy dance.
Your jokes are bright, they light up my day,
In the glow of your smile, I'm here to stay.

In a store, you trip, and I stifle a grin,
Navigating aisles, it's a win-win.
Your cart filled with snacks, oh what a sight,
With you by my side, everything feels right.

Unspoken words twinkle like stars,
In this cosmic dance, we dodge our guitars.
Every quirk is a beacon, lighting our way,
In the laughter we share, come what may.

As the sun dips low and shadows grow long,
We can't help but sing our silly song.
In the light that surrounds us, we happily twirl,
Two goofballs together, just giving it a whirl.

Melodies in Sweet Spaces

In the kitchen, we dance and twirl,
You trip on the cat, oh what a swirl!
Sizzling bacon meets a delightful squeak,
Laughter erupts, it's the highlight of the week.

Socks on our feet, we slide on the floor,
Music blasting, we always want more.
With every hiccup and joyful spin,
Together we laugh, let the fun begin!

We chase bubbles, watching them soar,
One pops too close, and we both roar.
Giggling like kids, we dive in the fun,
Who knew life's antics could make us run?

Late-night snacks turn into a feast,
With fries and ice cream, we just can't cease.
Stumbling through jokes, we again fall apart,
Each moment with you, a melody of heart.

Enchanted by Your Being

Your hair's a mess; what a glorious sight,
You make me laugh till the morning light.
Seeing you dance, what a curious sight,
You twirl and you trip, oh what a delight!

In the park, we skip, we jump, we tease,
Your attempts at grace bring me to my knees.
The way you pout when you munch your cake,
Each funny face is a precious keepsake.

You sing off-key, but I love the rhyme,
You steal the last fry, but I think it's fine.
Chasing you down for a tickle or two,
In this mad dance, it's always just you.

Your laugh's like music, it fills the air,
With you by my side, I couldn't care.
In our little world, we create our tune,
A symphony of joy that makes gloom swoon.

The Essence of Us

Your jokes are wild, your puns so great,
They linger long past that first dinner plate.
In silly debates on the best pizza pie,
We laugh and we argue, oh me, oh my!

You snort when you laugh; it's a sound to hear,
Like a funny trumpet so near and dear.
With tickles and giggles, we spar like two bears,
Life's a circus, but we don't care.

Chasing the dog while he runs with our sock,
Each moment we share feels like a tick-tock.
In the rain, we splash in our brightly-colored shoes,
Every puddle's a stage where we sing out our blues.

With silly faces and wild little games,
We find our joy, and we never feel shame.
In our quirky bubble, we thrive and we sway,
Together in laughter, come what may.

Traces of Your Light

On lazy mornings, you mess up the sheets,
With cereal and laughter, we make funny beats.
You spill your coffee in a grand ballet,
A splash zone of joy to start the day!

You tell a joke, and I nearly choke,
Who knew your humor could set off a smoke?
In the silliness, we find pure delight,
Like two goofy stars in the soft twilight.

With every surprise, you add to the glow,
From paper planes to our wild, silly flow.
In shadows and giggles, we wander the night,
Spinning in chaos, everything feels right.

The way you smile, with mischief ablaze,
Turns mundane moments into a playful craze.
Through laughter, we leap, dance through the scenes,
In the traces of you, found in our dreams.

A Canvas of Us

Your laugh, like a brush, paints my day,
Each giggle a splash, in a bright ballet.
We dance on clouds, in a silly parade,
Chasing sunbeams, in this colorful shade.

You say I'm a mess, in my mismatched socks,
But who needs perfection when fun never blocks?
With crayons of chaos, we sketch out our dreams,
In this masterpiece, nothing's quite as it seems.

Your puns are like glitter, they sprinkle the air,
Transforming my frown into bursts of fresh flair.
With you by my side, each mishap's a joke,
Our laughter a canvas where joy never broke.

Life's a funny sketch with wild, crazy hues,
I'll paint it with laughter, with all of my clues.
So here's to the art, chaotic yet true,
A canvas of giggles, forever with you.

Timeless Interludes

In a world unhinged, we find our own rhyme,
Like spoons in a drawer, we're lost in our time.
You crack up my mornings, my evenings, my nights,
Like mismatched socks, we're hilarious sights.

Our chats are like popcorn, they pop and they burst,
In the cinema of life, we're both well rehearsed.
With silly debates on who's better at food,
Each laugh is a tune in this joyful mood.

Tick-tock, can't stop—our clocks play a song,
In this timeless dance, you can't be wrong.
You juggle my worries, you trip on my fears,
But we laugh 'til the sun sets and brings forth the cheers.

As shadows grow long, let's skip down the lane,
With whimsical thoughts that we'll never restrain.
In the theater of moments, forever we'll glide,
You and I, a duet, with laughter our guide.

The Air We Share

With each quip a bubble, we float through the day,
Like two silly bubbles, we giggle and sway.
In the air we breathe, there's a whirlwind of cheer,
Silly thoughts fly like kites, when you're near.

You sneeze, I erupt—what a comical show,
In the breeze, we share all our odd little flow.
Your puns are like breezes, that make my heart race,
We're the odd pair, who just can't find their place.

Clouds of laughter surround us, we soar through the mist,
I'll catch your weird dance—how could I resist?
We play tag with giggles, in a rollicking air,
Breathless with joy, without any care.

Floating on giddy, we leave trails of fun,
With pranks and with jokes, we've only just begun.
In the sky of our whimsy, we'll make our own glares,
A world filled with laughter, in the air that we share.

Moments Like Drops of Rain

We splash through the puddles, oh, what a delight,
Every drop is a giggle, bursting in flight.
Like mischievous raindrops, we dance in the glow,
In a symphony of whimsy, our laughter will flow.

You point at the clouds, and we shape them in glee,
"Is that really a whale or just a lost tee-hee?"
Each moment's a raindrop, a tickle, a tease,
We're wet with our laughter, you and me, if you please.

As lightning strikes laughter, we dive into pools,
Dancing with droplets, two joy-ridden fools.
With each thundered chuckle, sky-high we will sway,
Playing hide-and-seek with the clouds on display.

So here's to the moments, like soft drops of rain,
In this silly story, we'll always remain.
With puddles of fun, and sunshine as our fame,
Laughing through storms, we'll never feel shame.

Echoing Emotions

You laughed and snorted, oh what a sound,
Your goofy grin goes around and around.
With each little hiccup, my heart does bounce,
In this clumsy dance, we still can pounce.

We trip over shoes and bump into walls,
Your silly faces make me break into falls.
Who needs a stage when we have this space?
Together we shine, a comical race.

Our humor's a bond, as tight as a knot,
In this circus of life, you're the jester I sought.
With pranks in the air, and jokes flying free,
You paint my gray skies, oh how bright we can be.

So here's to our laughter, the echoing cheer,
In this joke-filled tale, I'm glad that you're near.
Through chuckles and giggles, we'll always survive,
In this dance of the silly, we truly thrive.

Caresses of the Universe

The stars sometimes giggle, when we look up high,
We make funny wishes, just you and I.
As planets collide, and comets pass through,
We spin in our orbits, not knowing what's due.

Your lazy nods make the cosmos collide,
My silly antics, like a wild cosmic ride.
With each rolling star, we burst out in glee,
In the arms of the universe, we dance like the sea.

Planets will wobble when you shake your head,
Neptune is jealous, he wishes instead.
We twirl in the stardust, with sparkles and light,
Our laughter's the melody that carries the night.

So let's chase the meteors that streak through the sky,
With our arms flailing wide, like kids we will fly.
In this cosmic ballet, we'll find our own tune,
With the universe laughing, under the late moon.

Tides of Shared Dreams

The waves crash with giggles, as you splash right in,
Each droplet a chuckle, where do we begin?
We ride on our boogie boards, making a scene,
The sun is our spotlight, and we are the queen.

With pails full of sand, we build castles that sway,
Soon taken by the tides, "It's your fault!" I say.
We throw seashells at seagulls, who steal our snacks,
In this ocean of laughter, there's nothing that lacks.

With each wave that rises, we float and we sink,
Your silly faces make me pause and rethink.
As tides surge and fall, there's magic in sight,
Every splash a memory, from morning till night.

Together we'll swim, through ripples and dreams,
In this tide of the silly, nothing's as it seems.
We laugh 'til we cry, in this watery scheme,
Through the swells of our fortune, we flow like a stream.

In the Embrace of Love

Your pretend to snooze, while I sneak a bite,
The cookie jar's empty, oh what a sight!
But your playful smirk makes it all worth the gain,
In our sweet little chaos, there's never a chain.

We dance in the kitchen, our socks slip and slide,
Making pancakes together, it's more like a ride.
The syrup is sticky, you get it in my hair,
With each sugary mishap, we float without care.

Your goofy expressions are straight from a clown,
With silly impressions, you'll never back down.
We giggle and argue, it's all in good fun,
In this hilarious saga, we shine like the sun.

So here's to our days, filled with laughter and cheer,
In this cuddly embrace, I'm glad you are here.
With silly adventures and hugs that are tight,
Our love is a riot, a true pure delight.

Chasing the Dawn Together

We sprint at dawn, like goofy fools,
With hair like birds' nests, breaking rules.
You trip, I laugh, the sun starts to rise,
Oblivious to the sleepy skies.

Coffee spills as we race to the park,
Dogs bark loudly, they sense the spark.
With each sip, we make silly vows,
To spin in circles, and not see cows.

Our giggles echo in morning's light,
As we dodge pigeons in awkward flight.
You catch my hand, our balance sways,
Together we dance through the sun's warm rays.

Chasing the dawn, our hearts are bold,
In this silly game, love's purest gold.
With laughter and joy, we'll never stop,
In every sunrise, our spirits hop.

Embrace of the Gentle Breeze

In the park we picnic, ants join the feast,
You toss me a sandwich, I squeal like a beast.
The breeze wraps around us, tickles our ears,
We giggle like children, forgetting our fears.

You wear that hat, two sizes too large,
I push it down, declaring, "I'm in charge!"
With silly faces and butterfly nets,
Chasing our shadows without any regrets.

A kite gets tangled, we wrestle it free,
It soars like our laughter, wild as can be.
You catch my eye, and we burst out in song,
Off-key and loud, but our hearts sing along.

As we sway in the breeze, we both feel the thrill,
Each moment of laughter gives time a new chill.
With crumbs on our cheeks and hearts full of cheer,
We embrace the wind, with nothing to fear.

Love's Sweet Cadence

You tap your feet, I dance like a clown,
Twirl like a whirlwind, taking a bow down.
The rhythm we make is a comical beat,
With snorts and giggles, we shuffle our feet.

In parking lots, we start our parade,
With shopping carts as drums, we serenade.
As we march through aisles with silly precision,
Our playlist's a mashup of pure indecision.

Every wrong note, a memory made,
Our life's a dance, where joy won't fade.
Twisting and turning to laughter's own song,
In this waltz of love, we can't go wrong.

Our hearts beat like music, light and bright,
In the cadence of laughter, we take flight.
With every misstep, our bond starts to grow,
In this love symphony, we steal the show.

The Rhythm of Our Souls

You hum a tune that I can't quite place,
I jump in, offbeat, with a silly face.
Our laughter syncs, like a quirky drum,
As we dance in the kitchen, oh how we become!

With flour on noses and sugar in hair,
We bake up a storm, without a care.
You crack a joke, and the cookies burn bright,
But our giggles keep going, through day and night.

We swipe at the spatula, waging a war,
It's a friendly skirmish, with joy at the core.
Our harmony blooms like flowers in spring,
In the rhythm of laughter, we'll dance and we'll sing.

As we shimmy through life, with quirks in our steps,
In each little moment, love silently preps.
So here's to the tune that plays in our hearts,
In the rhythm of us, that laughter imparts.

The Touch of You

Your elbows knock against my side,
Like two clumsy penguins on a ride.
We giggle loud, it must look weird,
But oh, the joy is truly cleared.

Your hand's a squirrel on the loose,
I swear it thinks it's got a truce.
It tickles me, I squeak and squeal,
In this dance, we spin and reel.

With every poke, we start to laugh,
Counting the times that you just gaff.
The silly games that we both play,
Make dreary moments fade away.

So here's to slips and laughter bright,
When life feels wrong, we make it right.
In playful jests, our hearts renew,
What better magic? The touch of you.

Sails of Shared Dreams

We set our sails on munchy cheese,
Riding waves of giggles with ease.
Your voice, a wind, it fills me up,
Like sailing seas in a giant cup.

Tacos sing while dolphins dance,
We float along in a crazy trance.
Your laughter bubbles like champagne,
As seagulls join our wild refrain.

With chocolate maps and jellybeans,
Our treasure hunts are silly scenes.
Two pirates lost but never meek,
In shared dreams, it's fun we seek.

So hoist the flags, let's sail away,
In our own world, forever stay.
On sails of laughter, out we go,
To where the silly breezes blow.

Discords that Unite

We argue over where to eat,
Like cats and dogs who miss a beat.
You want the burger, I want pie,
In our chaos, we both just sigh.

But in the midst of heated debate,
You crack a joke, and I can't wait.
We burst out laughing, all is good,
Those silly fights, misunderstood.

Like mismatched socks or two left shoes,
We duke it out, then sip our brews.
In every squabble, there's delight,
Our frenzied dance is pure insight.

So here's to clashes, loud and bright,
That twist and turn, then spark the light.
For in this chaos, love takes flight,
Discords that unite feel so right.

Serenity in Your Gaze

Your eyes are pools of silly dreams,
In them, life glows, or so it seems.
When you just stare and crack a grin,
I'm lost in thoughts of where we've been.

Your laughter dances in the air,
With every glance, there's love to share.
A wink from you can brighten days,
Like sunshine lost in funny ways.

Together, we make quite the sight,
Clumsiness wrapped in pure delight.
With each twinkle, I find my way,
In soothing calm, your eyes convey.

So here's my heart, take a peruse,
In your sweet gaze, I cannot lose.
In this serenity, truth lays,
In you, I find my silliest ways.

www.ingramcontent.com/pod-product-compliance
Ingram Content Group UK Ltd.
Pitfield, Milton Keynes, MK11 3LW, UK
UKHW020123171224
452675UK00014BA/1546